I0015215

Python Programming for Beginners

An easy guide to learn python
programming language for
absolute beginners.

by

Marco Robert

This document is geared towards providing exact and reliable information in regards to the topic and issue covered. The publication is sold with the idea that the publisher is not required to render accounting, officially permitted, or otherwise, qualified services. If advice is necessary, legal or professional, a practiced individual in the profession should be ordered.

- From a Declaration of Principles which was accepted and approved equally by a Committee of the American Bar Association and a Committee of Publishers and Associations.

The information provided herein is stated to be truthful and consistent, in that any liability, in terms of inattention or otherwise, by any usage or abuse of any policies, processes, or directions contained within is the solitary and utter responsibility of the recipient reader. Under no circumstances will any legal responsibility or blame be held against the publisher for any reparation, damages, or monetary loss due to the information herein, either directly or indirectly.

Respective authors own all copyrights not held by the publisher.

The information herein is offered for informational purposes solely, and is universal as so. The presentation of the information is without contract or any type of guarantee assurance.

The trademarks that are used are without any consent, and the publication of the trademark is without permission or backing by the trademark owner. All trademarks and brands within this book are for clarifying purposes only and are the owned by the owners themselves, not affiliated with this document.

Disclaimer and Terms of Use: The Author and Publisher has strived to be as accurate and complete as possible in the creation of this book, notwithstanding the fact that he does not warrant or represent at any time that the contents within are accurate due to the rapidly changing nature of the Internet. While all attempts have been made to verify information provided in this publication, the Author and Publisher assumes no responsibility for errors, omissions, or contrary interpretation of the subject matter herein.

Any perceived slights of specific persons, peoples, or organizations are unintentional. In practical advice books, like anything else in life, there are no guarantees of results. Readers are cautioned to rely on their own judgment about their individual circumstances and act accordingly.

This book is not intended for use as a source of legal, medical, business, accounting or financial advice. All readers are advised to seek services of competent professionals in the legal, medical, business, accounting, and finance fields.

Table of Contents

Introduction to Python Programming

The programming language you will be learning is Python. Python is an example of a high-level language; other high-level languages you might have heard of are C++, PHP, and Java.

As you might infer from the name high-level language, there are also low-level languages, sometimes referred to as machine languages or assembly languages. Machine language is the encoding of instructions in binary so that they can be directly executed by the computer. Assembly language uses a slightly easier format to refer to the low level instructions. Loosely speaking, computers can only execute programs written in low-level languages. To be exact, computers can actually only execute programs written in machine language. Thus, programs written in a high-level language (and even those in assembly language) have to be processed before they can run. This extra processing takes some time, which is a small disadvantage of high-level languages. However, the advantages to high-level languages are enormous.

First, it is much easier to program in a high-level language. Programs written in a high-level language take less time to write, they are shorter and easier to read, and they are more likely to be correct. Second, high-level languages are portable, meaning that they can run on different kinds of computers with few or no modifications. Low-level programs can run on only one kind of computer and have to be rewritten to run on another.

Due to these advantages, almost all programs are written in high-level languages. Low-level languages are used only for a few specialized applications.

Two kinds of programs process high-level languages into low-level languages: interpreters and compilers. An interpreter reads a high-level program and executes it, meaning that it does what the program says. It processes the program a little at a time, alternately reading lines and performing computations.

A compiler reads the program and translates it completely before the program starts running. In this case, the high-level program is called the source code, and the translated program is called the object code or the executable. Once a program is compiled, you can execute it repeatedly without further translation.

Many modern languages use both processes. They are first compiled into a lower level language, called byte code, and then interpreted by a program called a virtual machine. Python uses both processes, but because of the way programmers interact with it, it is usually considered an interpreted language.

There are two ways to use the Python interpreter: shell mode and program mode. In shell mode, you type Python expressions into the Python shell, and the interpreter immediately shows the result. The example below shows the Python shell at work.

```
$ python3
Python 3.2 (r32:88445, Mar 25 2011, 19:28:28)
[GCC 4.5.2] on linux2
Type "help", "copyright", "credits" or "license" for
more information.
>>> 2 + 3
5
>>>
```

The >>> is called the Python prompt. The interpreter uses the prompt to indicate that it is ready for instructions. We typed 2 + 3. The interpreter evaluated our expression and replied 5. On the next line it gave a new prompt indicating that it is ready for more input.

Working directly in the interpreter is convenient for testing short bits of code because you get immediate feedback. Think of it as scratch paper used to help you work out problems.

Alternatively, you can write an entire program by placing lines of Python instructions in a file and then use the interpreter to execute the contents of the file as a whole. Such a file is often referred to as source code. For example, we used a text editor to create a source code file named firstprogram.py with the following contents:

```
print("My first program adds two numbers, 2 and 3:")
print(2 + 3)
```

By convention, files that contain Python programs have names that end with .py . Following this convention will help your operating system and other programs identify a file as containing python code.

```
$ python firstprogram.py
My first program adds two numbers, 2 and 3:    5
```

These examples show Python being run from a Unix command line. In other development environments, the details of executing programs may differ. Also, most programs are more interesting than this one.

What Are the Important Reasons to Learn the Python Programming Language?

Python is an open-source and high-level programming language developed for use with a broad range of operating systems. It is termed as most powerful programming language due to its dynamic and diversified nature. Python is easy-to-use with simple syntax and people who learn it for the first time find it very easy to grab the concepts.

Having used by pioneer websites such as YouTube, Drop Box, Python has high demand in the market. If you would want to get the benefit of Python, register to Python Training.

Let's now learn the important reasons due to which Python language is used at a wider range of people.

* Object Oriented Programming
One of the powerful tools of Python is Object Oriented Programming, which allows data structures creation and reusability. Due to this reusability, the work is done efficiently and reduces a lot of time. During recent years, object oriented programming pertains to classes and many interactive objects. Object Oriented Programming techniques can be used in any of the software and can be implemented in any of the programming languages.

* Readability

With the simple syntax, the python coding language is very easy to understand. Hence, Python can be used as a prototype and can be implemented in other programming language after testing the code.

* Python is free

As Python is an open-source programming language, it is free of cost and allow unrestricted use. With this open-source license, it can be modified, redistributed and used commercially. The license is available even for entire source code with cost free support. CPython, the most widely used implementation of Python, can be used in all operating systems. Being the well designed, robust software with scalable and portable capabilities has become a widely used programming language.

Programming at a faster rate

Python is a high-level language and when programming using this language is quite faster when compared to the execution time done using the other low level languages.

Cross-platform operating ability

Python can be executed on all the major operating systems such as Mac OS, Microsoft Windows, Linus, and Unix. This programming language gives the best experience to work with any of the OS.
Integration Capabilities

Following are the notable integration capabilities of Python:

* Process control capabilities are powerful
* Ability to be embedded as scripting programming language
* Easy to develop web services
* Helps to implement many internet protocols

If you interested to work with Python, register into one of the Python Training Institute where the candidates get more benefits out of the training. For information see, Python Training. Highly talented and professional faculties take the training sessions for the aspirants get a good understanding. Aspirants can check their understanding level with the help of the mock tests available online. Accurate test results will be given in the form of analytical reports. The aspirants can also opt for the other learning solutions such as corporate training, Boot camp training, classroom training etc.

Python Overview

Python is a clear and powerful object-oriented programming language, comparable to Perl, Ruby, Scheme, or Java.

Python is a high-level, structured, open-source programming language that can be used for a wide variety of programming tasks. Python was created by Guido Van Rossum in the early 1990s; its following has grown steadily and interest has increased markedly in the last few years or so. It is named after Monty Python's Flying Circus comedy program.

Python is used extensively for system administration (many vital components of Linux distributions are written in it); also, it is a great language to teach programming to novices. NASA has used Python for its software systems and has adopted it as the standard scripting language for its Integrated Planning System. Python is also extensively used by Google to implement many components of its Web Crawler and Search Engine & Yahoo! for managing its discussion groups.

Python within itself is an interpreted programming language that is automatically compiled into bytecode before execution (the bytecode is then normally saved to disk, just as automatically, so that compilation need not happen again until and unless the source gets changed). It is also a dynamically typed language that includes (but does not require one to use) object-oriented features and constructs.

The most unusual aspect of Python is that whitespace is significant; instead of block delimiters (braces → "{}" in the C family of languages), indentation is used to indicate where blocks begin and end.

For example, the following Python code can be interactively typed at an interpreter prompt, display the famous "Hello World!" on the user screen:

```
>>> print "Hello World!"
Hello World!
```

Another great feature of Python is its availability for all platforms. Python can run on Microsoft Windows, Macintosh and all Linux distributions with ease. This makes the programs very portable, as any program written for one platform can easily be used on another.

Python provides a powerful assortment of built-in types (e.g., lists, dictionaries and strings), a number of built-in functions, and a few constructs, mostly statements. For example, loop constructs that can iterate over items in a collection instead of being limited to a simple range of integer values. Python also comes with a powerful standard library, which includes hundreds of modules to provide routines for a wide variety of services including regular expressions and TCP/IP sessions.

Python is used and supported by a large Python Community that exists on the Internet. The mailing lists and news groups like the tutor list actively support and help new python programmers. While they discourage doing homework for you, they are quite helpful and are populated by the authors of many of the Python textbooks currently available on the market.

Python Environment Set Up

One of the most important things you'll do when working with any programming language is setup a development environment which allows you to execute the code you write. Without this, you will never be able to check your work and see if your website or application is free of syntax errors.

With Python, you also need something called an interpreter that converts your code - which makes up the entirety of your application - to something the computer can read and execute. Without this interpreter, you'll have no way to run your code.

To convert your code, you must first use a Python shell, which calls upon the interpreter through something called a "bang" line.

As for creating an application or file, there are two ways to do this. You can create a program using a simple text editor like WordPad, or Notepad++. You can also create a program using a Python shell. There are advantages and disadvantages to each method, which we'll discuss next.

Python Shell versus Text File

A shell is a program or tool that can be used to interact with a system. For instance, the Windows operating system shell can be tapped into by using a "terminal" or command line to submit commands and arguments.

With Python, things work a bit differently than an operating system shell. The Python shell is used to interact with an interpreter, which feeds code to a computer in a form that it can understand.

When you execute a Python program that you've written, the interpreter reads the code and converts it into usable commands.
The important thing to note is that all of this is done after the program has been executed.

With a shell, the interpreting - or conversion - happens in real-time as you type the code into the computer or system. This means that the actual program is executing as you type. This gives you some idea of how your final code will look, and what your program is actually going to do.

When you write code in a text file, none of that happens until you feed the document into an interpreter. If you have Python installed on your computer you can call upon the interpreter using a command line, but this step is done after you've already written the code.

This makes it more difficult to spot errors in your code, and it can also be frustrating if the interpreter runs into issues, because they may not be as apparent as they would if you had used a shell. Still, a lot of developers prefer to use a text editing tool because it is simple and easy to do.

There are text editors with increased functionality - like Notepad++ - which were specifically developed with programming in mind.

The Best Place to Start

Before you can do anything with a programming language, you first need to configure the development environment. Now, we're going to cover how to setup Python and the interpreter that will execute your custom programs.

Python comes pre-installed on Mac and a majority of Linux distributions. However, you may need to download an updated version depending on how old your system is.

TIP: You can easily check your Python version by opening the terminal and running the following command:

python -V

 Windows Installation
Here are the steps to install Python on Windows machine.

Open a Web browser and go to https://www.python.org/downloads/.

Follow the link for the Windows installer python-XYZ.msi file where XYZ is the version you need to install.

To use this installer python-XYZ.msi, the Windows system must support Microsoft Installer 2.0. Save the installer file to your local machine and then run it to find out if your machine supports MSI.

Run the downloaded file. This brings up the Python install wizard, which is really easy to use. Just accept the default settings, wait until the install is finished, and you are done.

Macintosh Installation

Recent Macs come with Python installed, but it may be several years out of date.

See http://www.python.org/download/mac

for instructions on getting the current version along with extra tools to support development on the Mac. For older Mac OS's before Mac OS X 10.3 (released in 2003), MacPython is available.

Jack Jansen maintains it and you can have full access to the entire documentation at his website – http://www.cwi.nl/~jack/macpython.html. You can find complete installation details for Mac OS installation.

Setting up PATH

Programs and other executable files can be in many directories, so operating systems provide a search path that lists the directories that the OS searches for executables.

The path is stored in an environment variable, which is a named string maintained by the operating system. This variable contains information available to the command shell and other programs.

The path variable is named as PATH in Unix or Path in Windows (Unix is case sensitive; Windows is not).

In Mac OS, the installer handles the path details. To invoke the Python interpreter from any particular directory, you must add the Python directory to your path.

Setting path at Unix/Linux

To add the Python directory to the path for a particular session in Unix –

In the csh shell – type setenv PATH "$PATH:/usr/local/bin/python" and press Enter.

In the bash shell (Linux) – type export ATH="$PATH:/usr/local/bin/python" and press Enter.

In the sh or ksh shell – type
PATH="$PATH:/usr/local/bin/python" and press
Enter.

Note – /usr/local/bin/python is the path of the
Python directory

Setting path at Windows
To add the Python directory to the path for a
particular session in Windows –

At the command prompt – type path
%path%;C:\Python and press Enter.

Note – C:\Python is the path of the Python directory

Running Python
There are three different ways to start Python –

Interactive Interpreter
You can start Python from Unix, DOS, or any other
system that provides you a command-line interpreter
or shell window.

Enter python the command line.

Start coding right away in the interactive interpreter.

$python # Unix/Linux
or
python% # Unix/Linux

or

C:> python # Windows/DOS

Here is the list of all the available command line options –

Sr.No. Option & Description

1

-d

It provides debug output.

2

-O

It generates optimized bytecode (resulting in .pyo files).

3

-S

Do not run import site to look for Python paths on startup.

4

-v

verbose output (detailed trace on import statements).

5

-X

disable class-based built-in exceptions (just use strings); obsolete starting with version 1.6.

6
-c cmd

run Python script sent in as cmd string

7
file

run Python script from given file

Script from the Command-line
A Python script can be executed at command line by invoking the interpreter on your application, as in the following –

$python script.py # Unix/Linux

or

python% script.py # Unix/Linux

or

C: >python script.py # Windows/DOS
Note – Be sure the file permission mode allows execution.

Integrated Development Environment
You can run Python from a Graphical User Interface (GUI) environment as well, if you have a GUI application on your system that supports Python.

Unix – IDLE is the very first Unix IDE for Python.

Windows – PythonWin is the first Windows interface for Python and is an IDE with a GUI.

Macintosh – The Macintosh version of Python along with the IDLE IDE is available from the main website, downloadable
as either MacBinary or BinHex'd files.

If you are not able to set up the environment properly, then you can take help from your system admin. Make sure the Python
environment is properly set up and working perfectly fine.

Note – All the examples given in subsequent chapters are executed with Python 2.4.3 version available on CentOS flavor of
Linux.

Python Basic Syntax

Here, you will learn about basic syntax of a python program. Basic syntax of a python program is too simple than other languages. Let's take an example, here the following program prints "Hello Python, I am Python Basic Syntax" as output:

```
# Python Basic Syntax - Example Program
print("Hello Python, I am Python Basic Syntax");
```

Let's take another example demonstrating basic syntax of Python language.

```
print("This is,\nPython basic syntax\nExample");
print("You will learn all about Python");
```

Case Sensitivity

All variables are case-sensitive. Python treats 'number' and 'Number' as separate, unrelated entities.

Spaces and tabs don't mix

Instead of block delimiters (braces → "{}" in the C family of languages), indentation is used to indicate where blocks begin and end. Because whitespace is significant, remember that spaces and tabs don't mix, so use only one or the other when indenting your programs. A common error is to mix them. While they may look the same in editor, the interpreter will read them differently and it will result in either an error or unexpected behavior. Most decent text editors can be configured to let tab key emit spaces instead.

Python's Style Guideline described that the preferred way is using 4 spaces.

Crystal Clear action bookmark.png

Tips: If you invoked python from the command-line, you can give -t or -tt argument to python to make python issue a warning or error on inconsistent tab usage.

This will issue an error if you have mixed spaces and tabs.

Objects
In Python, like all object-oriented languages, there are aggregations of code and data called objects, which typically represent the pieces in a conceptual model of a system.

Objects in Python are created (i.e., instantiated) from templates called classes (which are covered later, as much of the language can be used without understanding classes). They have attributes, which represent the various pieces of code and data which make up the object. To access attributes, one writes the name of the object followed by a period (henceforth called a dot), followed by the name of the attribute.

An example is the 'upper' attribute of strings, which refers to the code that returns a copy of the string in which all the letters are uppercase. To get to this, it is necessary to have a way to refer to the object (in the following example, the way is the literal
string that constructs the object).

'bob'.upper
Code attributes are called methods. So in this example, upper is a method of 'bob' (as it is of all strings). To execute the code in a method, use a matched pair of parentheses surrounding a comma separated list of whatever arguments the method accepts (upper doesn't accept any arguments). So to find an uppercase version of the string 'bob', one could use the following:

'bob'.upper()
Scope

In a large system, it is important that one piece of code does not affect another in difficult to predict ways. One of the simplest ways to further this goal is to prevent one programmer's choice of a name from blocking another's use of that name. The concept of scope was invented to do this. A scope is a "region" of code in which a name can be used and outside of which the name cannot be easily accessed. There are two ways of delimiting regions in Python: with functions or with modules. They each have different ways of accessing from outside the scope useful data that was produced within the scope. With functions, that way is to return the data. The way to access names from other modules leads us to another concept.

Namespaces

It would be possible to teach Python without the concept of namespaces because they are so similar to attributes, which we have already mentioned, but the concept of namespaces is one that transcends any particular programming language, and so it is important to teach. To begin with, there is a built-in function dir() that can be used to help one understand the concept of namespaces. When you first start the Python interpreter (i.e., in interactive mode), you can list the objects in the current (or default) namespace using this function.

```
Python 2.3.4 (#53, Oct 18 2004, 20:35:07) [MSC
v.1200 32 bit (Intel)] on win32
Type "help", "copyright", "credits" or "license" for
more information.
>>> dir()
['__builtins__', '__doc__', '__name__']
```
This function can also be used to show the names available within a module's namespace. To

demonstrate this, first we can use the type() function to show what kind of object __builtins__ is:

```
>>> type(__builtins__)
<type 'module'>
```

Since it is a module, it has a namespace. We can list the names within the __builtins__ namespace, again using the dir() function (note that the complete list of names has been abbreviated):

```
>>> dir(__builtins__)
['ArithmeticError', ... 'copyright', 'credits', ... 'help', ... 'license', ... 'zip']
>>>
```

Namespaces are a simple concept. A namespace is a particular place in which names specific to a module reside. Each name within a namespace is distinct from names outside of that namespace. This layering of namespaces is called scope. A name is placed within a namespace when that name is given a value. For example:

```
>>> dir()
['__builtins__', '__doc__', '__name__']
>>> name = "Bob"
>>> import math
>>> dir()
['__builtins__', '__doc__', '__name__', 'math', 'name']
```

Note that I was able to add the "name" variable to the namespace using a simple assignment statement. The import statement was used to add the "math" name to the current namespace. To see what math is, we can simply:

```
>>> math
<module 'math' (built-in)>
```

Since it is a module, it also has a namespace. To display the names within this namespace, we:

```
>>> dir(math)
['__doc__', '__name__', 'acos', 'asin', 'atan', 'atan2', 'ceil', 'cos', 'cosh', 'degrees', 'e',
'exp', 'fabs', 'floor', 'fmod', 'frexp', 'hypot', 'ldexp', 'log', 'log10', 'modf', 'pi', 'pow',
'radians', 'sin', 'sinh', 'sqrt', 'tan', 'tanh']
>>>
```

If you look closely, you will notice that both the default namespace and the math module namespace have a '__name__' object. The fact that each layer can contain an object with the same name is what scope is all about. To access objects inside a namespace, simply use the name of the module, followed by a dot, followed by the name of the object. This allows us to differentiate between the __name__ object within the current namespace, and that of the object with the same name within the math module. For example:

```
>>> print (__name__)
__main__
>>> print (math.__name__)
math
```

```
>>> print (math.__doc__)
```
This module is always available. It provides access to the mathematical functions defined by the C standard.
```
>>> math.pi
3.1415926535897931
```

When we consider a Java program, it can be defined as a collection of objects that communicate via invoking each other's methods. Let us now briefly look into what do class, object, methods, and instance variables mean.

Object – Objects have states and behaviors. Example: A dog has states - color, name, breed as well as behavior such as wagging their tail, barking, eating. An object is an instance of a class.

Class – A class can be defined as a template/blueprint that describes the behavior/state that the object of its type supports.

Methods – A method is basically a behavior. A class can contain many methods. It is in methods where the logics are written, data is manipulated and all the actions are executed.

Instance Variables – Each object has its unique set of instance variables. An object's state is created by the values assigned to these instance variables.

First Java Program

Let us look at a simple code that will print the words Hello World.

Example

```java
public class MyFirstJavaProgram {

  /* This is my first java program.
   * This will print 'Hello World' as the output
   */

  public static void main(String []args) {
    System.out.println("Hello World"); // prints Hello World
  }
}
```

Let's look at how to save the file, compile, and run the program. Please follow the subsequent steps –

Open notepad and add the code as above.

Save the file as: MyFirstJavaProgram.java.

Open a command prompt window and go to the directory where you saved the class. Assume it's C:\.

Type 'javac MyFirstJavaProgram.java' and press enter to compile your code. If there are no errors in your code, the command prompt will take you to the next

line (Assumption : The path variable is set).
Now, type ' java MyFirstJavaProgram ' to run your program.

You will be able to see ' Hello World ' printed on the window.

Output
C:\> javac MyFirstJavaProgram.java
C:\> java MyFirstJavaProgram
Hello World
Basic Syntax

About Java programs, it is very important to keep in mind the following points.

Case Sensitivity – Java is case sensitive, which means identifier Hello and hello would have different meaning in Java.

Class Names – For all class names the first letter should be in Upper Case. If several words are used to form a name of the class, each inner word's first letter should be in Upper Case.

Example: class MyFirstJavaClass

Method Names – All method names should start with a Lower Case letter. If several words are used to form the name of the method, then each inner word's first letter should be in Upper Case.

Example: public void myMethodName()

Program File Name – Name of the program file should exactly match the class name.

When saving the file, you should save it using the class name (Remember Java is case sensitive) and append '.java' to the end of the name (if the file name and the class name do not match, your program will not compile).

Example: Assume 'MyFirstJavaProgram' is the class name. Then the file should be saved as 'MyFirstJavaProgram.java'

public static void main(String args[]) – Java program processing starts from the main() method which is a mandatory part of every Java program.

Java Identifiers

All Java components require names. Names used for classes, variables, and methods are called identifiers.

In Java, there are several points to remember about identifiers. They are as follows –

All identifiers should begin with a letter (A to Z or a to z), currency character ($) or an underscore (_).

After the first character, identifiers can have any

combination of characters.

A key word cannot be used as an identifier.

Most importantly, identifiers are case sensitive.

Examples of legal identifiers: age, $salary, _value, __1_value.

Examples of illegal identifiers: 123abc, -salary.

Java Modifiers
Like other languages, it is possible to modify classes, methods, etc., by using modifiers. There are two categories of modifiers
–
Access Modifiers – default, public , protected, private

Non-access Modifiers – final, abstract, strictfp

We will be looking into more details about modifiers in the next section.

Java Variables
Following are the types of variables in Java –

Local Variables
Class Variables (Static Variables)
Instance Variables (Non-static Variables)
Java Arrays

Arrays are objects that store multiple variables of the same type. However, an array itself is an object on the heap. We will look into how to declare, construct, and initialize in the upcoming chapters.

Java Enums
Enums were introduced in Java 5.0. Enums restrict a variable to have one of only a few predefined values. The values in this enumerated list are called enums.

With the use of enums it is possible to reduce the number of bugs in your code.

For example, if we consider an application for a fresh juice shop, it would be possible to restrict the glass size to small, medium, and large. This would make sure that it would not allow anyone to order any size other than small, medium, or large.

Example
 Live Demo
```
class FreshJuice {
  enum FreshJuiceSize{ SMALL, MEDIUM, LARGE }
  FreshJuiceSize size;
}
```

```
public class FreshJuiceTest {

  public static void main(String args[]) {
    FreshJuice juice = new FreshJuice();
    juice.size = FreshJuice.FreshJuiceSize.MEDIUM ;
```

```
    System.out.println("Size: " + juice.size);
  }
}
```

The above example will produce the following result –

Output

Size: MEDIUM

Note – Enums can be declared as their own or inside a class. Methods, variables, constructors can be defined inside enums

as well.

Python - Variable Types

Variables and Types

Python is completely object oriented, and not "statically typed". You do not need to declare variables before using them, or declare their type. Every variable in Python is an object.

This tutorial will go over a few basic types of variables.

Numbers
Python supports two types of numbers - integers and floating point numbers. (It also supports complex numbers, which will not be explained in this tutorial).

To define an integer, use the following syntax:

```
script.py
IPythin Shell
1 myint = 7
print(myint)https://www.learnpython.org/en
2 /Variables_and_Types
```

To define a floating point number, you may use one of the following notations:

```
script.py

1 myfloat = 7.0
```

2 print(myfloat)

3 myfloat = float(7)

4 print(myfloat)

Strings

Strings are defined either with a single quote or a double quotes.

script.py

1 mystring = 'hello'

2 print(mystring)

3 mystring = "hello"

4 print(mystring)

The difference between the two is that using double quotes makes it easy to include apostrophes (whereas these would terminate the string if using single quotes)

mystring = "Don't worry about apostrophes"
print(mystring)

There are additional variations on defining strings

that make it easier to include things such as carriage returns, backslashes and Unicode characters. These are beyond the scope of this tutorial, but are covered in the Python documentation.

Simple operators can be executed on numbers and strings:

script.py

```
1 one = 1

2 two = 2

3 three = one + two

4 print(three)

5
6 hello = "hello"

7 world = "world"

8 helloworld = hello + " " + world

9 print(helloworld)
```

A variable provides us with named storage that our programs can manipulate. Each variable in Java has a specific type, which determines the size and layout of the variable's memory; the range of values that can be stored within that memory; and the set of operations that can be applied to the variable.

You must declare all variables before they can be used. Following is the basic form of a variable declaration –

data type variable [= value][, variable [= value] ...] ;
Here data type is one of Java's datatypes and variable is the name of the variable. To declare more than one variable of the specified type, you can use a comma-separated list.

Following are valid examples of variable declaration and initialization in Java –

Example
int a, b, c;   // Declares three ints, a, b, and c.
int a = 10, b = 10; // Example of initialization
byte B = 22;   // initializes a byte type variable B.
double pi = 3.14159; // declares and assigns a value of PI.
char a = 'a';   // the char variable a iis initialized with value 'a'

Local Variables

Local variables are declared in methods, constructors, or blocks.

Local variables are created when the method,

41

constructor or block is entered and the variable will be destroyed once it exits the method, constructor, or block.

Access modifiers cannot be used for local variables.

Local variables are visible only within the declared method, constructor, or block.

Local variables are implemented at stack level internally.

There is no default value for local variables, so local variables should be declared and an initial value should be assigned before the first use.

Example
Here, age is a local variable. This is defined inside pupAge() method and its scope is limited to only this method.

```
public class Test {
  public void pupAge() {
    int age = 0;
    age = age + 7;
    System.out.println("Puppy age is : " + age);
  }

  public static void main(String args[]) {
    Test test = new Test();
    test.pupAge();
```

```
  }
}
```

This will produce the following result −

Output
Puppy age is: 7
Example
Following example uses age without initializing it, so it would give an error at the time of compilation.

```
public class Test {
  public void pupAge() {
    int age;
    age = age + 7;
    System.out.println("Puppy age is : " + age);
  }

  public static void main(String args[]) {
    Test test = new Test();
    test.pupAge();
  }
}
```

This will produce the following error while compiling it −

Output
Test.java:4:variable number might not have been initialized
age = age + 7;
      ^
1 error

Instance Variables

Instance variables are declared in a class, but outside a method, constructor or any block.

When a space is allocated for an object in the heap, a slot for each instance variable value is created.

Instance variables are created when an object is created with the use of the keyword 'new' and destroyed when the object is destroyed.

Instance variables hold values that must be referenced by more than one method, constructor or block, or essential parts of an object's state that must be present throughout the class.

Instance variables can be declared in class level before or after use.

Access modifiers can be given for instance variables.

The instance variables are visible for all methods, constructors and block in the class. Normally, it is recommended to make these variables private (access level). However, visibility for subclasses can be given for these variables with the use of access modifiers.

Instance variables have default values. For numbers, the default value is 0, for Booleans it is false, and for object references it is null. Values can be assigned during the declaration or within the constructor.

Instance variables can be accessed directly by calling the variable name inside the class. However, within static methods (when instance variables are given accessibility), they should be called using the fully qualified name.
ObjectReference.VariableName.

```
import java.io.*;
public class Employee {

  // this instance variable is visible for any child class.
  public String name;

  // salary  variable is visible in Employee class only.
  private double salary;

  // The name variable is assigned in the constructor.
  public Employee (String empName) {
    name = empName;
  }

  // The salary variable is assigned a value.
  public void setSalary(double empSal) {
    salary = empSal;
  }

  // This method prints the employee details.
  public void printEmp() {
```

```
      System.out.println("name  : " + name );
      System.out.println("salary :" + salary);
   }

   public static void main(String args[]) {
      Employee empOne = new Employee("Ransika");
      empOne.setSalary(1000);
      empOne.printEmp();
   }
}
```

This will produce the following result −

Output
name : Ransika
salary :1000.0
Class/Static Variables
Class variables also known as static variables are declared with the static keyword in a class, but outside a method,
constructor or a block.

There would only be one copy of each class variable per class, regardless of how many objects are created from it.

Static variables are rarely used other than being declared as constants. Constants are variables that are declared as public/private, final, and static. Constant variables never change from their initial value.

Static variables are stored in the static memory. It is rare to use static variables other than declared final and used as either public or private constants.

Static variables are created when the program starts and destroyed when the program stops.

Visibility is similar to instance variables. However, most static variables are declared public since they must be available for
users of the class.

Default values are same as instance variables. For numbers, the default value is 0; for Booleans, it is false; and for object references, it is null. Values can be assigned during the declaration or within the constructor. Additionally, values can be assigned in special static initializer blocks.

Static variables can be accessed by calling with the class name ClassName.VariableName.

When declaring class variables as public static final, then variable names (constants) are all in upper case. If the static variables are not public and final, the naming syntax is the same as instance and local variables.

Example
 Live Demo
import java.io.*;

```java
public class Employee {

  // salary  variable is a private static variable
  private static double salary;

  // DEPARTMENT is a constant
  public    static    final    String    DEPARTMENT    =
"Development ";

  public static void main(String args[]) {
    salary = 1000;
    System.out.println(DEPARTMENT    +    "average
salary:" + salary);
  }
}
```

Python - Basic Operators

Operators are special symbols in Python that carry out arithmetic or logical computation. The value that the operator operates on is called the operand.

For example:

>>> 2+3
5
Here, + is the operator that performs addition. 2 and 3 are the operands and 5 is the output of the operation.

Arithmetic operators

Arithmetic operators are used to perform mathematical operations like addition, subtraction, multiplication etc.

When you run the program, the output will be:

x + y = 19
x - y = 11
x * y = 60
x / y = 3.75
x // y = 3
x ** y = 50625

Comparison operators

Comparison operators are used to compare values. It either returns True or False according to the condition.

Comparision operators in Python

Operator Meaning Example
> Greater that - True if left operand is greater than the right x > y
< Less that - True if left operand is less than the right x < y
== Equal to - True if both operands are equal x == y
!= Not equal to - True if operands are not equal x != y
>= Greater than or equal to - True if left operand is greater than or equal to the right x >= y
<= Less than or equal to - True if left operand is less than or equal to the right

Logical operators

Logical operators are the and, or, not operators.

Logical operators in Python
Operator Meaning Example
and True if both the operands are true x and y
or True if either of the operands is true x or y
not True if operand is false (complements the operand) not x

Bitwise operators

Bitwise operators act on operands as if they were string of binary digits. It operates bit by bit, hence the name.

For example, 2 is 10 in binary and 7 is 111

Assignment operators
Assignment operators are used in Python to assign values to variables.

a = 5 is a simple assignment operator that assigns the value 5 on the right to the variable a on the left.

There are various compound operators in Python like a += 5 that adds to the variable and later assigns the same. It is equivalent to a = a + 5.

]Special operators
Python language offers some special type of operators like the identity operator or the membership operator. They are described below with examples.

Identity operators
is and is not are the identity operators in Python. They are used to check if two values (or variables) are located on the same part of the memory. Two variables that are equal does not imply that they are identical.

Identity operators in Python Operator Meaning Example

is True if the operands are identical (refer to the same object) x is True is not True if the operands are not identical (do not refer to the same object) x is not True

Python - Decision Making

The ability to make decisions based off of data is one of the most basic aspects of programming. Python, like most languages, does this via the 'if' statement:

```
if name=="Nick":
 print "Another name that begins with N!"
 n_names+=1
```

A single = in a statemnt is an assignment. Double == is a boolean statement. It compares whether the left side of the == and the right side are the same. If so, the block of code under it is executed. If not, it is skipped.

We can also compares numbers:

```
if age==100:
 print "Age has now reached triple digits!"
```

We can also compare a boolean:

```
if have_drivers_license==True:
 print "Can operate a car"
```

Comparative Operators
In addition to '==', there are several other comparative operators to use: >,<,<=,>=,!=, and 'not'

Extending the example from above, first we'll print

any name that begins with N through Z

:

```
if name>"N":
 print "Another name in the second half of the alphabet!"
 second_half_names+=1
```

Likewise, with numerical operations:

```
if age>9:
 print "Age is no longer single digits"
```

For readabiltiy's sake, we can use the >= to mean greater or equal to

```
if age>=10:
 print "Age is no longer single digits"
```

'<' and '<=' work in similar ways, meaning less than and less than or equal to respectively:

```
if name <"N":
 print "Another name in the first half of the alphabet"
 first_half_names+=1
```

```
if age<=9:
 print "Age is still single digits"
```

The '!=' operator means not equal to:

```
if have_drivers_license!=True:
 print "Not allowed to operate a car"
```

Given Python's tendendcy to use real words in expressions, we also can use the 'not' operator to negate a conditional
statement:

```
if not have_drivers_license==True:
 print "Not allowed to operate a car"
```

```
if not age>=10
 print "Age is still single digits
```

For integers, a variable is considered false if it's 0 and considered true otherwise. Therefore we can also test out some comparisons simply by:

```
done=0
if not done:  #if done==0
 print "Not finished yet"
done=1
if done: #if done!=0
 print "Finished"
```

Following the above, we can also shorten our boolean comparison since a boolean value will already be True or False.
There's no need for a == comparison:

```
have_drivers_license=True
```

```
if have_drivers_license:
    print "Can operate a car"

have_drivers_license=False
if not have_drivers_license:
    print "Can not operate a car"
```

Multiple Comparisons

All the above examples used very simple comparative statements. But what if you wanted to do multiple comparisons before executing a block of code? You could use nested if statements like:

```
if name=="John":
    if have_drivers_license:
        print "John has a driver's license"
```

But this can start to become unreadable. So, for multiple comparisons,we have the 'and' and 'or' operators. Python uses these keywords as a replacement for '&&' and '||' seen in other languages for readability sake. So, the above example can be rewritten as:

```
if name=="John" and have_drivers_license:
    print "John has a driver's license"
```

For the 'or' statement, to compare for two different items both hitting the same code block, we could do:
```
if name=="Nick":
```

```
    print "Another name that begins with N!"
    n_names+=1
if name=="Nate":
    print "Another name that begins with N!"
    n_names+=1
```

However, this is messy. Better to rewrite it with the 'or' keyword:

```
if name=="Nick" or name=="Nate":
 print "Another name that begins with N!"
 n_names+=1
```

For 'or' statements, the left hand side of the 'or' is always evaluated first. If it passes, the second one is never evaluated.

Using these simple keywords and operators we can generate complex conditional statements:

```
if (house_number>=1020 and house_number<=1380
and street_name=="Maple") or (houseNumber>=57
and
houseNumber<=280 and streetName=="Elm"):
 print "The house is close enough to current location"
```

In this example, if the first address matches, there's no need to check the second address
In
Sometimes, using multiple 'and' or 'or' can be tiring to type out. Consider:

```
if name=="Nick" or name=="Jen" or name="Amy" or
name=="Billy":
 collegeStudents+=1
```

What a mess. But by using the 'in' statement, we can clean it up a bit.

```
if name in ["Nick","Jen","Amy","Billy"]:
 collegeStudents+=1
```

Effectively, what we're doing here is creating an ad hoc list and checking whether the value of name is in the list. Therefore, we can also use the 'in' operator to quickly compare a value against the contents of any list:

```
if name in nameList:
 print "Found %s in the list!" % (name)
```

We can even use the 'in' keyword to clean up the house number example above

```
if    (house_number    in    range(1020,1380)    and
street_name=="Maple")    or    (house_number    in
range(57,280) and
streetName=="Elm")
 print "The house is close enough to current location"
```

The range function will be discussed more in Loops

Else and Elif

Of course, sometimes you want to specify an alternative block of code if your conditional statement doesn't pass. This is done
using the 'else' keyword:

```
if name>"N":
    print "Another name in the second half of the alphabet!"
    second_half_names+=1
else:
 print "Another name in the first half of the alphabet!"
 first_half_names+=1
```

Yes, we could do something like:

```
if name>"N":
    print "Another name in the second half of the alphabet!"
    second_half_names+=1

if name<"N":
    print "Another name in the first half of the alphabet!"
    first_half_names+=1
```

However, this means you need to do two comparisons and the prior example is simpler to read.

But what if you have a secondary comparison you need to do should the first one fail? In that case, we use 'elif' (a contraction of 'else if'):

```
if name in ["Nick","Jen","Amy","Billy"]:
    business_majors+=1
elif name in ["Lauren","Matt","Nate","Beth":
 finance_majors+=1
else:
 undeclared_majors+=1
```

Like above, making an 'elif' into a second 'if' would mean doing one more unnecessary comparison should the first
comparison pass

Python - Loops

To keep a computer doing useful work we need repetition, looping back over the same block of code again and again. This will describe the different kinds of loops in Python.

For Loop

The for loop that is used to iterate over elements of a sequence, it is often used when you have a piece of code which you want to repeat "n" number of time.

It works like this: " for all elements in a list, do this "

Let's say that you have a list
computer_brands = ["Apple", "Asus", "Dell", "Samsung"]
for brands in computer_brands: print brands

That reads, for every element that we assign the variable brands, in the list computer_brands, print out the variable brands
numbers = [1,10,20,30,40,50]
sum = 0
for number in numbers:
   sum = sum + numbers
print sum
for i in range(1,10):
   print i

Break

To break out from a loop, you can use the keyword "break".

```
for i in range(1,10):
    if i == 3:
   break
     print i
```

Continue

The continue statement is used to tell Python to skip the rest of the statements in the current loop block and to continue to the next iteration of the loop.

```
for i in range(1,10):
    if i == 3:
   continue
     print i
```

While Loop

The while loop tells the computer to do something as long as the condition is met it's construct consists of a block of code and a condition.

It works like this: " while this is true, do this "

```
computer_brands = ["Apple", "Asus", "Dell", "Samsung"]
i = 0
while i < len(computer_brands):
    print computer_brands(i)
    i = i + 1
```

That reads, as long as the value of the variable i is less than the length of the list (computer_brands), print out the variable name.

```
while True:
    answer = raw_input("Start typing...")
    if answer == "quit":
        break
    print "Your answer was", answer
```

Let's show another example.

Here we set the variable counter to 0.

For every time the while loop runs, the value of the counter is increased by 2.

The while loop will run as long as the variable counter is less or equal with 100.
```
counter = 0
while counter <= 100:
    print counter
    counter + 2
```

Nested Loops
In some script you may want to use nested loops.

A nested loop is a loop inside a loop.
```
for x in range(1, 11):
    for y in range(1, 11):
        print '%d * %d = %d' % (x, y, x*y)
```
for loops are traditionally used when you have a block of code which you want to repeat a fixed number of times. The Python for statement iterates over the members of a sequence in order, executing

the block each time. Contrast the for statement with the "while" loop, used when a condition needs to be checked each iteration, or to repeat a block of code forever. For example:

For loop from 0 to 2, therefore running 3 times.

```
for x in range(0, 3):
    print "We're on time %d" % (x)
```
While loop from 1 to infinity, therefore running forever.

```
x = 1
while True:
    print "To infinity and beyond! We're getting close, on %d now!" % (x)
    x += 1
```
As you can see, these loop constructs serve different purposes. The for loop runs for a fixed amount - in this case, 3, while the while loop runs until the loop condition changes; in this example, the condition is the boolean True which will never change, so it could theoretically run forever. You could use a for loop with a huge number in order to gain the same effect as a while loop, but what's the point of doing that when you have a construct that already exists? As the old saying goes, "why try to reinvent the wheel?".

How do they work?

If you've done any programming before, you have

undoubtedly come across a for loop or an equivalent to it. Many languages have conditions in the syntax of their for loop, such as a relational expression to determine if the loop is done, and an increment expression to determine the next loop value. In Python this is controlled instead by generating the appropriate sequence. Basically, any object with an iterable method can be used in a for loop. Even strings, despite not having an iterable method - but we'll not get on to that here. Having an iterable method basically means that the data can be presented in list form, where there are multiple values in an orderly fashion. You can define your own iterables by creating an object with next() and iter() methods. This means that you'll rarely be dealing with raw numbers when it comes to for loops in Python - great for just about anyone!

Nested loops

When you have a block of code you want to run x number of times, then a block of code within that code which you want to run y number of times, you use what is known as a "nested loop". In Python, these are heavily used whenever someone has a list of lists - an iterable object within an iterable object.

```
for x in xrange(1, 11):
    for y in xrange(1, 11):
        print '%d * %d = %d' % (x, y, x*y)
```

Early exits

Like the while loop, the for loop can be made to exit before the given object is finished. This is done using the break statement, which will immediately drop out of the loop and contine execution at the first statement after the block. You can also have an optional else clause, which will run should the for loop exit cleanly - that is, without breaking.

```
for x in xrange(3):
    if x == 1:
        break
Things to remember
range vs xrange
```

The "range" is seen so often in for statements that you might think range is part of the for syntax. It is not: it is a Python built-in function which returns a sequence, which meets the requirement of providing a sequence for the for statement to iterate over. In Python 2.x, range generates the entire sequence when called, while xrange is a generator - it produces values on demand, not all up fromt. You will often see xrange is used much more frequently than range. This is for one reason only - resource usage. For large sequences, the difference in memory usage can be considerable. xrange uses less memory, and should the for loop exit early, there's no need to waste time creating the unused numbers. This effect is tiny in smaller lists, but increases rapidly in larger lists as you can see in the examples below. For Python 3.x, range was changed, you can think of it as being equivalent to the Python 2.x xrange, which no longer is defined in Python 3.x.

Examples
For..Else

```
for x in xrange(3):
    print x
else:
    print 'Final x = %d' % (x)
```
Strings as an iterable

```
string = "Hello World"
for x in string:
    print x
```
Lists as an iterable

```
collection = ['hey', 5, 'd']
for x in collection:
    print x
```
Loop over Lists of lists

```
list_of_lists = [ [1, 2, 3], [4, 5, 6], [7, 8, 9]]
for list in list_of_lists:
    for x in list:
        print x
```

Creating your own iterable

```python
class Iterable(object):

    def __init__(self,values):
        self.values = values
        self.location = 0

    def __iter__(self):
        return self

    def next(self):
        if self.location == len(self.values):
            raise StopIteration
        value = self.values[self.location]
        self.location += 1
        return value
```

range vs xrange (Python 2)

```python
import time

#use time.time() on Linux

start = time.clock()
for x in range(10000000):
    pass
stop = time.clock()

print stop - start

start = time.clock()
for x in xrange(10000000):
    pass
stop = time.clock()
```

```
print stop - start
```
Time on small ranges

```
import time

#use time.time() on Linux

start = time.clock()

for x in range(1000):
    pass
stop = time.clock()

print stop-start

start = time.clock()
for x in xrange(1000):
    pass
stop = time.clock()

print stop-start
```
Your own range generator using yield

```
def my_range(start, end, step):
    while start <= end:
        yield start
        start += step

for x in my_range(1, 10, 0.5):
    print x
```

Python- Numbers

Number Data Type in Python

Python supports integers, floating point numbers and complex numbers. They are defined as int, float and complex class in Python.

Integers and floating points are separated by the presence or absence of a decimal point. 5 is integer whereas 5.0 is a floating point number.

Complex numbers are written in the form, x + yj, where x is the real part and y is the imaginary part.

We can use the type() function to know which class a variable or a value belongs to and isinstance() function to check if it belongs to a particular class.

```
1 a = 5

3 # Output: <class 'int'>

4 print(type(a))


5
6 # Output: <class 'float'>

7 print(type(5.0))
```

```
8
9 # Output: (8+3j)

10 c = 5 + 3j

11 print(c + 3)
12


13 # Output: True
14
print(isinstance(c, complex))
```

While integers can be of any length, a floating point number is accurate only up to 15 decimal places (the 16th place is inaccurate).

Numbers we deal with everyday are decimal (base 10) number system. But computer programmers (generally embedded programmer) need to work with binary (base 2), hexadecimal (base 16) and octal (base 8) number systems.

In Python, we can represent these numbers by appropriately placing a prefix before that number. Following table lists these prefix.

Number system prefix for Python numbers

Number System	Prefix

Binary	'Ob' or 'OB'
Octal	'Oo' or 'OO'
Hexadecimal	'Ox' or 'OX'

Here are some examples

1 # Output: 107

2 print(0b1101011)
3

4 # Output: 253 (251 + 2)

5 print(0xFB + 0b10)
6
7 # Output: 13

8 print(0o15)

When you run the program, the output will be:

107
253
13

Type Conversion

We can convert one type of number into another. This is also known as coercion.

Operations like addition, subtraction coerce integer to float implicitly (automatically), if one of the operand is float.

```
>>> 1 + 2.0
3.0
```

We can see above that 1 (integer) is coerced into 1.0 (float) for addition and the result is also a floating point number.

We can also use built-in functions like int(), float() and complex() to convert between types explicitly. These function can even convert from strings.

```
>>> int(2.3)
2
>>> int(-2.8)
-2
>>> float(5)
5.0
>>> complex('3+5j')
(3+5j)
```

When converting from float to integer, the number gets truncated (integer that is closer to zero).

Python Decimal

Python built-in class float performs some calculations that might amaze us. We all know that the sum of 1.1 and 2.2 is 3.3, but Python seems to disagree.

```
>>> (1.1 + 2.2) == 3.3
```

False

What is going on?

It turns out that floating-point numbers are implemented in computer hardware as binary fractions, as computer only understands binary (0 and 1). Due to this reason, most of the decimal fractions we know, cannot be accurately stored in our computer.

Let's take an example. We cannot represent the fraction 1/3 as a decimal number. This will give 0.33333333... which is infinitely long, and we can only approximate it.

Turns out decimal fraction 0.1 will result into an infinitely long binary fraction of 0.000110011001100110011... and our computer only stores a finite number of it.

This will only approximate 0.1 but never be equal. Hence, it is the limitation of our computer hardware and not an error in Python.

```
>>> 1.1 + 2.2
3.3000000000000003
```
To overcome this issue, we can use decimal module that comes with Python. While floating point numbers have precision up to 15 decimal places, the decimal module has user settable precision.

```
1 import decimal
2
3 # Output: 0.1
4 print(0.1)
5
6
```

```
# Output:
Decimal('0.1000000000000000055511151231257827
021181583404541015625')
```

```
7 print(decimal.Decimal(0.1))
```

This module is used when we want to carry out decimal calculations like we learned in school.

It also preserves significance. We know 25.50 kg is more accurate than 25.5 kg as it has two significant decimal places compared to one.

```
1 from decimal import Decimal as D
2
# Output: Decimal('3.3')
3
print(D('1.1') + D('2.2'))
4
5 # Output: Decimal('3.000')
6 print(D('1.2') * D('2.50'))
```

Python - Strings

What is String in Python?
A string is a sequence of characters.

A character is simply a symbol. For example, the English language has 26 characters.

Computers do not deal with characters, they deal with numbers (binary). Even though you may see characters on your screen, internally it is stored and manipulated as a combination of 0's and 1's.

This conversion of character to a number is called encoding, and the reverse process is decoding. ASCII and Unicode are some of the popular encoding used.

In Python, string is a sequence of Unicode character. Unicode was introduced to include every character in all languages and bring uniformity in encoding. You can learn more about Unicode from here.

How to create a string in Python?

Strings can be created by enclosing characters inside a single quote or double quotes. Even triple quotes can be used in Python but generally used to represent multiline strings and docstrings.

How to create a string in Python?

Strings can be created by enclosing characters inside a single quote or double quotes. Even triple quotes can be used in Python but generally used to represent multiline strings and docstrings.

script.py   IPython Shell

```
1 # all of the following are equivalent

2 my_string = 'Hello'

3 print(my_string)
4

5
my_string = "Hello"

6 print(my_string)


7
8 my_string = '''Hello'''

9 print(my_string)
10


11 # triple quotes string can extend multiple lines

12 my_string = """Hello, welcome to
```

```
13 the world of 14 Python"""
print(my_string)
```

When you run the program, the output will be:

```
Hello
Hello
Hello
Hello, welcome to
      the world of Python
```

How to access characters in a string?

We can access individual characters using indexing and a range of characters using slicing. Index starts from 0. Trying to access a character out of index range will raise an IndexError. The index must be an integer. We can't use float or other types, this will result into TypeError.

Python allows negative indexing for its sequences. The index of -1 refers to the last item, -2 to the second last item and so on. We can access a range of items in a string by using the slicing operator (colon).

```
1 str = 'programiz'

2 print('str = ', str)


3
```

```
4 #first character
5
print('str[0] = ', str[0])
```

```
6
7 #last character

print('str[-1] = ', str[-1])
```

```
9
10 #slicing 2nd to 5th character
11
print('str[1:5] = ', str[1:5])
```

```
12
13 #slicing 6th to 2nd last character

14 print('str[5:-2] = ', str[5:-2])
```

If we try to access index out of the range or use decimal number, we will get errors.

```
# index must be in range
>>> my_string[15]
...
IndexError: string index out of range
```

```
# index must be an integer
```

```
>>> my_string[1.5]
...
```
TypeError: string indices must be integers
Slicing can be best visualized by considering the index to be between the elements as shown below.

If we want to access a range, we need the index that will slice the portion from the string.

How to change or delete a string?

Strings are immutable. This means that elements of a string cannot be changed once it has been assigned. We can simply reassign different strings to the same name.

```
>>> my_string = 'programiz'
>>> my_string[5] = 'a'
...
```
TypeError: 'str' object does not support item assignment
```
>>> my_string = 'Python'
>>> my_string
'Python'
```

We cannot delete or remove characters from a string. But deleting the string entirely is possible using the keyword del.

```
>>> del my_string[1]
...
```

TypeError: 'str' object doesn't support item deletion
>>> del my_string
>>> my_string
...
NameError: name 'my_string' is not defined

Python String Operations

There are many operations that can be performed with string which makes it one of the most used datatypes in Python.

Concatenation of Two or More Strings
Joining of two or more strings into a single one is called concatenation.

The + operator does this in Python. Simply writing two string literals together also concatenates them.

The * operator can be used to repeat the string for a given number of times.

```
1 str1 = 'Hello'

2 str2 ='World!
3
4 '

# using +
5
print('str1 + str2 = ', str1 + str2)
```

81

```
6
7 # using *

8 print('str1 * 3 =', str1 * 3)
9
```

Writing two string literals together also concatenates them like + operator.

If we want to concatenate strings in different lines, we can use parentheses.

```
>>> # two string literals together
>>> 'Hello ''World!'
'Hello World!'

>>> # using parentheses
>>> s = ('Hello '
...      'World')
>>> s
'Hello World'
```

Iterating Through String

Using for loop we can iterate through a string. Here is an example to count the number of 'l' in a string.

```
1 count = 0
2
for letter in 'Hello World':

3     if(letter == 'l'):
```

4   count += 1

5 print(count,'letters found')

String Membership Test

We can test if a sub string exists within a string or not, using the keyword in.

```
>>> 'a' in 'program'
True
>>> 'at' not in 'battle'
False
```

P?thon list

The most basic data structure in Python is the sequence. Each element of a sequence is assigned a number - its position or index. The first index is zero, the second index is one, and so forth.

Python has six built-in types of sequences, but the most common ones are lists and tuples, which we would see in this tutorial.

There are certain things you can do with all sequence types. These operations include indexing, slicing, adding, multiplying, and checking for membership. In addition, Python has built-in functions for finding the length of a sequence and for finding its largest and smallest elements.

Python Lists
The list is a most versatile datatype available in Python which can be written as a list of comma-separated values (items) between square brackets. Important thing about a list is that items in a list need not be of the same type.

Creating a list is as simple as putting different comma-separated values between square brackets. For example –

```
list1 = ['physics', 'chemistry', 1997, 2000];
list2 = [1, 2, 3, 4, 5 ];
```

list3 = ["a", "b", "c", "d"]
Similar to string indices, list indices start at 0, and lists can be sliced, concatenated and so on.

Accessing Values in Lists
To access values in lists, use the square brackets for slicing along with the index or indices to obtain value available at that index. For example –

```
#!/usr/bin/python

list1 = ['physics', 'chemistry', 1997, 2000];
list2 = [1, 2, 3, 4, 5, 6, 7 ];
print "list1[0]: ", list1[0]
print "list2[1:5]: ", list2[1:5]
```
When the above code is executed, it produces the following result –

```
list1[0]:  physics
list2[1:5]:  [2, 3, 4, 5]
```
Updating Lists
You can update single or multiple elements of lists by giving the slice on the left-hand side of the assignment operator, and you can add to elements in a list with the append() method. For example –

```
#!/usr/bin/python

list = ['physics', 'chemistry', 1997, 2000];
print "Value available at index 2 : "
print list[2]
```

```
list[2] = 2001;
print "New value available at index 2 : "
print list[2]
```

Note − append() method is discussed in subsequent section.

When the above code is executed, it produces the following result −

```
Value available at index 2 :
1997
New value available at index 2 :
2001
```

Delete List Elements

To remove a list element, you can use either the del statement if you know exactly which element(s) you are deleting or the remove() method if you do not know. For example −

```
#!/usr/bin/python

list1 = ['physics', 'chemistry', 1997, 2000];
print list1
del list1[2];
print "After deleting value at index 2 : "
print list1
```

When the above code is executed, it produces following result −

```
['physics', 'chemistry', 1997, 2000]
After deleting value at index 2 :
```

['physics', 'chemistry', 2000]
Note – remove() method is discussed in subsequent
section.

In Python programming, a list is created by placing all
the items (elements) inside a square bracket [ ],
separated by commas.

It can have any number of items and they may be of
different types (integer, float, string etc.).

```
# empty list
my_list = []
```

```
# list of integers
my_list = [1, 2, 3]
```

```
# list with mixed datatypes
my_list = [1, "Hello", 3.4]
```
Also, a list can even have another list as an item. This
is called nested list.

```
# nested list
my_list = ["mouse", [8, 4, 6], ['a']]
```
How to access elements from a list?
There are various ways in which we can access the
elements of a list.

List Index
We can use the index operator [] to access an item in
a list. Index starts from 0. So, a list having 5 elements

will have index from 0 to 4.

Trying to access an element other that this will raise an IndexError. The index must be an integer. We can't use float or other types, this will result into TypeError.

Nested list are accessed using nested indexing.

```
1 my_list = ['p','r','o','b','e']

2 # Output: p

3 print(my_list[0])

4
5 # Output: o

6 print(my_list[2])
7
8

# Output: e

9 print(my_list[4])
10
11

# Error! Only integer can be used for indexing
12
# my_list[4.0]
```

```
13
14 # Nested List
15
n_list = ["Happy", [2,0,1,5]]


16
17 # Nested indexing
18
19

# Output: a

20 print(n_list[0][1])
21
22

# Output: 5

23 print(n_list[1][3])
```

Conne🔲ting Access to Python

Access is not really a database, it is a file format. Thus, programs that access it, access the file directly. This has several benefits for small projects, being file size and speed.

Most databases act as a gate keeper between your application and the data files. This also makes it unpractical for multi user environments.

The other nice thing about access is its user interface. A novice to easily manipulate and populate the data. The data entered can be used by python. An example project of mine was to make a chamber directory site. The chamber information is kept in an access database. A python program reads the database and constructs html files from it.

Python can then act as an ftp client and download the files directly to the web server.

The first part is to install win32 on your computer. This will allow python to talk to macros COM interface, which talks to Access.

In this example we will use the DAO interface. In order to talk to access, we will be using the following objects

DBEngine, (connects to a database file)

DbeDatabase - provides database functionality

DbeRecordset, manipulates databases tables, this is what we will used.

To start we will create a DBEngind object, which will create a DBEDatabase object from which we create our recordset object.

engine = win32com.client.Dispatch("DAO.DBEngine.36")

Next we will construct the database object

db=engine.OpenDatabase(r"your databases file name")

Now we will construct an object for a table within the databas.

table = db.OpenRecordset("select * from nameofyourtable")

The table, curtly points to the first record. We may display one of its text fields as follows, given the field name is first_name

Print table.Fields("first_name").Value.encode('utf-8')

We may display a number value by

Print table.Fields("street_number").Value

Now to get the values of the next record, we move the record pointer up by calling MoveNext

Db.MoveNext().

We may print out all the names in our table by

while not table.EOF

print
table.Fields("first_name").encode('utf8')table.MoveN
ext()
To add a new record we use the Add and Update methods of the record set object

table.Add()

table.Firlds('firstname').value="Ted'

table.Update.

Now to change the current record we use the Edit

table.edit()

table.Fields('firstname').value='fred'

table.Update()

A useful property I find is Bookmark; it saves or sets a record position.

To boot mark the current record position

MyBookMark=table.Bookmark

Later on we may return to this record by

Table.Bookmark=MyBookMark.

Sometimes is may be useful to know how may records our object has. This is done by the RecordCount property. To display how many records our table has,

Print table.RecordCount

Now we may want to delete one of the records in the table, this is accomplish by

table.Delete()

Let's say we want to delete the record we just crested with Add.

table.Move Previous()

table.Delete()

Django Hosting and Python Hosting

Tools developed by online communities become really powerful and efficient today. They allow developers to work more efficiently and faster. Django is a good example of the platform that allows programmers and developers to create applications without waste of time. Just a couple lines of code in Django allow you to create a blog, gallery, or even a content management system for your website. The Django frameworkis also easy and quick way to learn the Python programming language as well as rapid development.

Django is based on Python and it is normally used for higher speed and design flexibility, as well as for developing a wide range of applications.

As a programming language, Python is quite popular among developers. And the Django framework astonishes anyone by its well organized package, useful and structured system templates and the overall simplicity.

Code Organization in Python

While the process ofapplication development in Python you will have to strictly follow the formatting and margins. The way you develop and format your programming code defines the application's logics. Of course, you will have to get used the first time. However in future anyone who knows the Python programming language will be able to easily navigate through your programming code in the same way as if it were his/her own project. Python is a perfect choice for team development.

Django Templates System

The templates system in Django is one of the most useful on the web development and programming market. With no problem, you can use conditional statements and cycles to manipulate complex data structures, which in its turn is very thoroughly described in the Django documentation for the convenience of use.

User-Friendly & Easy-To-Use

Python itself is a universal language of high-level programming where you can write simple console programs as well as complete cross-platform applications with GUI interfaces. Once some solution is written, it can easily be used as the basis for the next functionality development. At the same time, you can specify what parts / functions will be used in the code or not. But when developing web applications using the Django framework, the development process becomes much faster, more manageable and sets you free from lots of routine work such as the size of input fields for a form, type verification in form fields, authorization, sessions, etc. This allows you to get more focused on the logics of the application you develop.

Django Hosting

Django is usually provided by professional web hosting provider as a part of Python hosting. Combined django and python hosting provides plenty of opportunities to developers who can fully enjoy the robust and powerful functionality of the Django framework.

The Evolution of Python Language Over the Years

According to several websites, Python is one of the most popular coding languages of 2018. Along with being a high-level and general-purpose programming language, Python is also object-oriented and open source. At the same time, a good number of developers across the world have been making use of Python to create GUI applications, websites and mobile apps. The differentiating factor that Python brings to the table is that it enables programmers to flesh out concepts by writing less and readable code. The developers can further take advantage of several Python frameworks to mitigate the time and effort required for building large and complex software applications.

The programming language is currently being used by a number of high-traffic websites including Google, Yahoo Groups, Yahoo Maps, Linux Weekly News, Shopzilla and Web Therapy. Likewise, Python also finds great use for creating gaming, financial, scientific and educational applications. However, developers still use different versions of the programming language. According to the usage statistics and market share data of Python posted on W3techs, currently Python 2 is being used by 99.4% of websites, whereas Python 3 is being used only by 0.6% of websites. That is why, it becomes essential for each programmer to understand different versions of Python, and its evolution over many years.

How Python Has Been Evolving over the Years?

Conceived as a Hobby Programming Project

Despite being one of the most popular coding languages of 2015, Python was originally conceived by Guido van Rossum as a hobby project in December 1989. As Van Rossum's office remained closed during Christmas, he was looking for a hobby project that will keep him occupied during the holidays. He planned to create an interpreter for a new scripting language, and named the project as Python. Thus, Python was originally designed as a successor to ABC programming language. After writing the interpreter, Van Rossum made the code public in February 1991. However, at present the open source programming language is being managed by the Python Software Foundation.

Version 1 of Python

Python 1.0 was released in January 1994. The major release included a number of new features and functional programming tools including lambda, filter, map and reduce.

The version 1.4 was released with several new features like keyword arguments, built-in support for complex numbers, and a basic form of data hiding. The major release was followed by two minor releases, version 1.5 in December 1997 and version 1.6 in September 2000. The version 1 of Python lacked the features offered by popular programming languages of the time. But the initial versions created a solid foundation for development of a powerful and futuristic programming language.

Version 2 of Python

In October 2000, Python 2.0 was released with the new list comprehension feature and a garbage collection system. The syntax for the list comprehension feature was inspired by other functional programming languages like Haskell. But Python 2.0, unlike Haskell, gave preference to alphabetic keywords over punctuation characters. Also, the garbage collection system effectuated collection of reference cycles. The major release was followed by several minor releases. These releases added a number of functionality to the programming language like support for nested scopes, and unification of Python's classes and types into a single hierarchy. The Python Software Foundation has already announced that there would be no Python 2.8. However, the Foundation will provide support to version 2.7 of the programming language till 2020.

Version 3 of Python

Python 3.0 was released in December 2008. It came with a several new features and enhancements, along with a number of deprecated features. The deprecated features and backward incompatibility make version 3 of Python completely different from earlier versions. So many developers still use Python 2.6 or 2.7 to avail the features deprecated from last major release. However, the new features of Python 3 made it more modern and popular. Many developers even switched to version 3.0 of the programming language to avail these awesome features.

Python 3.0 replaced print statement with the built-in print() function, while allowing programmers to use custom separator between lines. Likewise, it simplified the rules of ordering comparison. If the operands are not organized in a natural and meaningful order, the ordering comparison operators can now raise a TypeError exception. The version 3 of the programming language further uses text and data instead of Unicode and 8-bit strings. While treating all code as Unicode by default it represents binary data as encoded Unicode.

As Python 3 is backward incompatible, the programmers cannot access features like string exceptions, old-style classes, and implicit relative imports. Also, the developers must be familiar with changes made to syntax and APIs. They can use a tool called "2to3" to migrate their application from

Python 2 to 3 smoothly. The tool highlights incompatibility and areas of concern through comments and warnings. The comments help programmers to make changes to the code, and upgrade their existing applications to the latest version of programming language.

Latest Versions of Python

At present, programmers can choose either version 3.4.3 or 2.7.10 of Python. Python 2.7 enables developers to avail improved numeric handling and enhancements for standard library. The version further makes it easier for developers to migrate to Python 3. On the other hand, Python 3.4 comes with several new features and library modules, security improvements and CPython implementation improvements. However, a number of features are deprecated in both Python API and programming language.

The developers can still use Python 3.4 to avail support in the longer run.

Version 4 of Python

Python 4.0 is expected to be available in 2023 after the release of Python 3.9. It will come with features that will help programmers to switch from version 3 to 4 seamlessly.

Also, as they gain experience, the expert Python developers can take advantage of a number of backward compatible features to modernize their existing applications without putting any extra time and effort. However, the developers still have to wait many years to get a clear picture of Python 4.0. However, they must monitor the latest releases to easily migrate to the version 4.0 of the popular coding language.

The version 2 and version 3 of Python are completely different from each other. So each programmer must understand the features of these distinct versions, and compare their functionality based on specific needs of the project. Also, he needs to check the version of Python that each framework supports. However, each developer must take advantage of the latest version of Python to avail new features and long-term support.

Getting Started with Python

Python is a computer programming language that lets you work more quickly than other programming languages. This tutorial will help you to become a python developer.

Getting started

To get started, you will need the Python interpreter or a Python IDE. An IDE is a tool that will make the experience of software development much better.

Python interpreter

You can download Python interpreter here: https://www.python.org/downloads/

The Python interpreter is a command line program, we'll discuss it in the next lecture.

Python programs are simply a collection of text files. If you want something more sophisticated than notepad for editing, you will need a Python IDEs (recommend). A Python IDE will make programming Python easier.

Python IDE

An IDE generally supports listing all program files, syntax highlighting and other features. There are lots of Python IDEs you could choose from.

Using one of these Python IDEs makes programming easier than in say, notepad. It will automatically color the text like the example below:

REPL

What is REPL?

REPL is the language shell.

Its short for Read, Eval, Print and Loop.
To start the language shell, type 'python' and press enter.

```
$ python
Python 3.6.1 (default, Mar 27 2017, 01:39:26)
[GCC 6.3.1 20170306] on linux
Type "help", "copyright", "credits" or "license" for
more information.
>>> 700713 + 700713 # read, eval
1401426 # print
>>> # loop
```

Then it starts this process:

1. Read: take user input.
2. Eval: evaluate the input.
3. Print: shows the output to the user.
4. Loop: repeat.

REPL

We can type all kinds of input in the interactive shell:

```
>>> 128 / 8
16.0
>>> 8 * (8 * 8)
512
>>> 256 * 4
1024
>>>
```

If you get an error when typing Python, install Python or set your environment variables. The method for setting this varies per operating system.

How to run

Learn how to run Python code?

You can execute Python code from the terminal or from a Python IDE. An IDE is a graphical environment that assitsts in software development.

All Python programs are written in code, text files with lots of instructions. These are saved with the extension .py.

Note: Often a Python program is not just one file, but many files.

To run a Python program, you need to have Python installed.

Python installed?

Open a terminal and type:

python file.py
where file.py is the name of your program. If you have more than one file, the main program is often the name of the program itself;

Use an IDE
Sometimes an easier way to execute Python programs is using a Python IDE. In a Python IDE, you simply press the 'play' button.

Python IDE
Python IDE : a software development tool. Compare Python IDEs.

An integrated software developent (IDE) makes software development much better!

Code with tabs, syntax highlighting, code completion and many awesome features!

Python IDEs

A list of the most popular Python IDEs. These are some of the most popular.
If you are a total beginer, I recommend PyCharm or

Spyder.

PyCharm

JetBrains Product
Free/Commercial
Closed-source
Linux, Mac and Windows support
Code Completion, Debugging, Bracket Matching, Line Numbering, Code Folding, Code Templates, Unit Testing, Integrated DB support.
Easy for beginners
Vim
Free
Open source
Cross platform, but mainly used on Linux
Works in terminal and over SSH (remote)
Code Completion, Debugging, Bracket Matching, Line Numbering, Code Folding, Code Templates, Unit Testing, Integrated DB support.
Hard for beginners
Spyder IDE

Free
Open source
Made for scientific programming
Windows, Linux, Mac support
Code Completion, Debugging, Bracket Matching, Line Numbering, Code Folding.

Wing IDE

Commercial
Closed-source
Cross platform
Code Completion, Debugging, Bracket Matching, Line Numbering, Code Folding, Code Templates, Unit Testing, Integrated DB support.
Sublime Text

Commercial/Free
Closed-source
Cross platform
Text editor for code and markup.
Polished interface, syntax highlighting, tabs.
Code Completion, Debugging, Bracket Matching, Line Numbering, Code Folding, Code Templates.

Emacs

Open source
Cross platform, but mainly Linux
Takes time to master
Works in terminal and over SSH
Code Completion, Debugging, Bracket Matching, Line Numbering, Code Folding, Code Templates, Unit Testing, Integrated DB support.

Text output

we can output to the terminal with print function. In this article we'll show you how to output text to the screen with Python.

Output

To output text to the screen you will need one line of code:

```
print("Hello World")
```

If you run the program:

Hello World
Print newline

To write multiple lines, add the '\n' character:

```
print("Hello World\nThis is a message")
```

Results in:

Hello World
This is a message
Note: the characters \n create a new line

Print variables
To print variables:

```
x = 3
print(x)
```

This will show:

3

To print multiple variables on one line:

```
x = 2
y = 3
print("x = {}, y = {}".format(x,y))
```

Will give you:

```
x = 2, y = 3
```

Text Input

Want to get keyboard input?

To get keyboard input, use the input function.

The input function has a return variable. In this case the keyboard input. If we do not store the return variable into a programs variable, we lose it. That's why we write a variable to store the result in.

User Input
To get a text value:

```
name = input("Enter a name: ")
print(name)
```

This will show you:

Enter a name:
You can now give keyboard input, it will be stored in the variable name.

Note: don't forget to store the return variable. variable = input("..")

Numeric input
To get a whole number:

```
x = int(input("What is x? "))
```

To get a decimal number:

```
x = float(input("Write a number"))
```

Strings

Strings in Python can be defined using quote symbols. An example of a string definition and output below:

```
s = "Hello World"
print(s)
```

This will output to the terminal:

Hello World

Accesing array elements

You may access character elements of a string using the brackets symbol, which are [and]. We do so by specifying the string name and the index.

Note: Computers start counting from zero, thus s[0] is the first character.

The example below prints the first element of a string.

```
print(s[0])
```

To print the second character you would write:

```
print(s[1])
```

String Slicing

You can slice the string into smaller strings. To do so you need to specify either a starting, ending index or both. Let us illustrate that in the Python shell:

```
>>> s = "Hello World"
>>> s[:3]
'Hel'
>>> s[3:]
'lo World'
>>> s[1:3]
'el'
>>>
```

If no number is given, such as in s[:3] it will simply take the beginning or end of teh string. We have accessed the string as if it was an array.

If you want to output them from your program, you have to wrap them in the print command. You can store the sliced string as a new string:

slice = s[0:5]

There you have it! String slicing is pretty easy.

Split string

Want to split a string?

To split a string, we use the method .split().

This method will return one or more new strings. All substrings are returned in the list datatype.

Note: Split with the method str.split(sep, maxsplit). The 2nd parameter is optional. If maxsplit is set, it returns no more than maxsplit elements.

String split

We can split a string based on a character.

s = "To convert the result to"

```
parts = s.split(" ")
print(parts)
```

Result:

```
['To', 'convert', 'the', 'result', 'to']
```
Any character can be used. If you want to get sentences you could use:

```
s = "Python string example. We split it using the dot character."
parts = s.split(".")
print(parts)
```

This will result in:

```
['Python string example', ' We split it using the dot character', '']
```

If statements

If statements are all about choices.

A block of code is executed based on one or more conditions. The block of code will only be executed if the condition is true.

If statements

Computer programs do not only execute instructions. Occasionally, a choice needs to be made. Such as a

114

choice is based on a condition.

Python has several conditional operators:

> greater than
< smaller than
== equals
!= is not

Conditions are always combined with variables. A program can make a choice using the if keyword. For example:

```
x = int(input("Tell X"))

if x == 4:
    print('You guessed correctly!')

print('End of program.')
```

The condition is shown on line 3.

When you execute this program it will always print 'End of program', but the text 'You guessed correctly!' will only be printed if the variable x equals to four.

Note: Code is executed based on the variable x. Try different numbers: 2,3,4

If else

Python can also execute a block of code if x does not equal to 4. The else keyword is used for that.

```
x = int(input("Tell X"))

if x == 4:
    print('You guessed correctly!')
else:
    print('Wrong guess')

print('End of program.')
```

If x is set to 2, the second code block is executed. If x equals (==) four, the first code block is executed.

if elif and else

We can chain if statements.

How?

Using the keywords elif and else. That way, we can walk through all options for the condition. Imagine a weather app: if snow, elif rain, elif thunder, else sunny. We can execute different code for each condition.

If elif and else

We can execute blocks of code using if-statements.

We can also do that if we have multiple conditions.

Lets start with an if statement, like so:

```
x = 3

if x < 5:
    print('x smaller than 5')
else:
    print('x is too big')
```

It will make the decision based on the value of x, also known as the condition.

```
x smaller than 5
```
What if you want to have multiple cases?
In that case you can use elif

```
x = 8

if x < 5:
    print('x smaller than 5')
elif x >= 5 and x <= 10:
    print('great choice')
else:
    print('x is too big')
```

Booleans

What is a boolean?

A boolean is a variable that is either True or False. We say the datatype of a variable can be booelan.

You can think of it like a light switch, its either on or off.

Note: A bit is the smallest unit in a computer. Its either 0 or 1, True or False. Also called a boolean

Boolean

To define a boolean in Python we simply type:

light = FALSE

If you want to set it to on, you would type:

light = TRUE

You can also type:

light = 0

which is equivalent to FALSE. Likewise you can write

light = 1

which is the same as TRUE.

Variables

Variables in Python can hold text and numbers. For example:

```
x = 2
price = 2.5
word = 'Hello'
```

The variable names are on the left and the values on the right. Once a variable is assigned, it can be used in other places of the program.

In the example above, we have three variables: x, price and word.

Note: Variables may not contain spaces or special characters.

Text in variables

Text variables may be defined in 3 ways:
```
word = 'Hello'
word = "Hello"
word = '''Hello'''
```

The type depends on what you prefer.

Operators

Once defined variables can be replaced or modified:

```
x = 2
```

```
# increase x by one
x = x + 1

# replace x
x = 5
```

Python supports the operators +, -, / and * as well as brackets. Variables may be shown on the screen using the print statement.

```
x = 5
print(x)

y = 3 * x
print(y)

# more detailed output
print("x = " + str(x))
print("y = " + str(y))
```

The first output of the program above is simply the raw value of the variables. If you want to print a more detailed message like "x = 5", use the line 'print("x = " + str(x))'.

This str() function converts the numeric variable to text.

Global variables

What is the difference between global and local variables?

A global variable can be accessed anywhere in code. A local variable can only be used in a specific code block.

global variable example

We say the scope is global, it can be used in any function or location throughout the code.
In the example below we define a global variable, y amount lines of code later we can still use that variable.

```
x = 3
...
200 lines of code
...
print(x)
```

Note: In Python a global variable is always limited to the module. Thus, there is no global variable as there is in other programming languages. It's always within a module.

local variables

This is contrary to a local variable, which can only be

accessed in the local scope.
In the example below, x is a local variable..

```
def f(x):
   .. x can only be used here
```

If a variable is declared inside a function or loop, it's a local variable. Global variables are usually defined at the top of the code.

Best practice

Global variables are considered a bad practice because functions can have non-obvious behavior. Usually you want to keep functions small, staying within the size of the screen. If variables are declared everywhere throughout the code, it becomes less obvious to what the function does.

Tuples

A tuple is a collection that cannot be modified.

Variables can be of the datatype tuple. A tuple is defined using parenthesis.
If you want to change the data during program execution, use a list instead of a tuple.

Example
A tuple with one item (a comma is needed in the end):

x = (1,)

A tuple with multiple items:

x = (1,2,3,4)

Note: Even with one element, the comma is needed.

Accessing tuples

To access individual elements, we use square brackets. To print the first element (Python starts counting from zero):

print(x[0])

To print the second element:

print(x[1])

To print the last element, you can count from the back using the minus sign.

print(x[-1])

Dictionary

A dictionary in Python is a one to one mapping.

Every key points to a value, separated by a colon (:).

A dictionary is defined using curly brackets. The value left of the colon is called the key, the value right of the colon is called the value. Every (key,value) pair is separated by a comma.

Example
The example below creates a dictionary. Keys must be unique values, you can not use the same key twice. Values may or may not be unique.

```
k = { 'EN':'English', 'FR':'French' }
print(k['EN'])
```

We defined a dictionary named k and access elements using the square brackets you've seen before. We use the key ['EN'] to print the value 'English'.

English
Note: A dictionary has no specific order.
Add and remove
To add a new value to a dictionary you can simply assign a key value pair:

```
k['DE'] = 'German'
```

To remove a key/value pair use the del keyword:

```
k = { 'EN':'English', 'FR':'French' }
```

```
del k['FR']
```

print(k)

Lists

A list is a collection of objects

Everything in Python is an object. These objects in a list are numbers in most cases. Lists can also contain text (strings) or both.

Note: Lists can have zero or more elements (empty lists are possible).

Lists Example

A list is defined using square brackets. Let us define as simple list:

c   = [5,2,10,48,32,16,49,10,11,32,64,55,34,45,41,23,26,27 ,72,18]

In this case we have a list defined by the variable c. We defined a purely random set of numbers above.

Accessing elements

To access individual elements, we use the same brackets. To print the first element (Python starts counting from zero):

```
print(c[0])
```

This shows

5

To print the second element:

```
print(c[1])
```

Results in:

2

To print the last element, you can count from the back using the minus sign.

```
print(c[-1])
```

Result

18

Size of the list
You can get the length of the list using the len function. Example code:

```
c = [5,2,10,48,32,16,49,10,11,32,64,55,34,45,41,23,26,27,72,18]
print(len(c))
```

Datatypes

List may contain various types of variables in the same list including text, whole numbers, floating point numbers and so on. For example, we may define a list with text
variables:

fears = ["Spiders","Ghosts","Dracula"]

List comprehensions

What is list comprehension?

List comprehensions are an easy way to create lists.

Its much easier to write a one liner than it is to write a for loop, just for creating a list. This one liner is called a list comprehension.

Example
Assume we want to create a list containing 100 numbers. Manually that would be a lot of typing work. So we would use a for loop, right?

We can define a for loop to fill the list.
numbers = []

for i in range(0,100):

```
numbers.append(i)
```

```
print(numbers)
```

We can replace it with a one liners, which is how we obtain the same result:

```
numbers = [ x for x in range(100) ]
```

This is also useful if you want to create large lists.

Note: List comprehensions can include function calls and expressions.

Assume we want the square roots to 100:

```
import math
```

```
numbers = [ math.sqrt(x) for x in range(100) ]
print(numbers)
```

For loops

Do you want to repeat code blocks?

To repeat code, the for keyword can be used.

Sometimes you need to execute a block of code more than once, for loops solve that problem. We specify the start and end of the loop using the function range(min,max).

Example
To execute a line of code 10 times we can do:

```
for i in range(1,11):
    print(i)
```

The last number (11) is not included. This will output the numbers 1 to 10. Python itself starts counting from 0, so this code will also work:

```
for i in range(0,10):
    print(i)
```

but will output 0 to 9.

The code is repeated while the condition is True. In this case the condition is: i < 10. Every iteration (round), the variable i is updated.

Nested loops
Loops can be combined:

```
for i in range(0,10):
    for j in range(0,10):
        print(i,' ',j)
```

In this case we have a multidimensional loops. It will iterate over the entire coordinate range (0,0) to (9,9)

While loop

Unsure how many times to repeat code?

Python has the while keyword. Unlike the for loop which tests the condition first, the while loop execute the code first. Sometimes we don't know how long sometimes will take.

A theoretical program could be (pseudocode):

```
while sun_not_shining:
  use jacket
  use gloves
```

which keeps executing the code block until the condition is true.

while loop example
Lets build an extended 'guess the number game':

```
x = 0
while x != 5:
  x = int(input("Guess a number:"))

  if x != 5:
    print("Incorrect choice")

print("Correct")
```

This will keep asking a number until the number is guessed. This is defined in the line: while x != 5, or in English, "while x is not equal to five, execute".

The program keeps repeating the code block while the condition (x!=5) is True. Once x equals 5, the program continues.

Infinite loops

If a condition in a while loop is never met, it could cause the program to run forever or to freeze/crash.

Functions

If you want to reuse code, you can use a function.

This prevents you from writing the same thing over and over again.

A function has a unique distinct name in the program. Once you call a function it will execute one or more lines of codes, which we will call a code block.

Function example
For example, we could have the Pythagoras function.

In case your math is a little rusty, $a^2 + b^2 = c^2$. Thus, c = sqrt($a^2 + b^2$). In code we could write that as:

```
import math

def pythagoras(a,b):
    value = math.sqrt(a *a + b*b)
    print(value)


pythagoras(3,3)
```

We call the function with parameters a=3 and b =3 on the last line. A function can be called several times with varying parameters. There is no limit to the number of function calls.

Note: The def keyword tells Python we define a function. Always use four spaces to indent the code block, using another number of spaces will throw a syntax error.

Return value

It is also possible to store the output of a function in a variable. To do so, we use the keyword return.

```
import math

def pythagoras(a,b):
    value = math.sqrt(a*a + b*b)
    return value


result = pythagoras(3,3)
print(result)
```

The function pythagoras is called with a=3 and b=3. The program execution continues in the function pythagoras. The output of math.sqrt(a*a + b*b) is stored in the function variable value. This is returned and the output is stored in the variable result. Finally, we print variable result to the screen.

Try except

Sometimes code throws an exception.

You can catch that exception using the try-except block.

The try-except statement starts with a block of code, and a response is specified in case an exception is thrown.

Note: In other programming languages this is often called try-catch.

Try-except example

Lets say we want to get numeric input from the keyboard and calculate the number squared.

The straight forward method would be:

```
# get keyboard input (string)
rawInput = input('Enter number:')
```

```
# convert string to integer
x = int(rawInput)
```

```
# calculate number squared
print(x*x)
```

This works as long as we give numeric input. If we would type "two", the program crashes – an exception is thrown. That's where try-catch comes in:

```
rawInput = input('Enter number:')
```

```
try:
    x = int(rawInput)
    print(x*x)
```

```
except:
```

```
    print('Invalid input specified')
```

We can also be specific about the type of exception we want to catch:

```
except ValueError:
```

```
    print('Invalid input specified')
```

Expanded For Loop

What is an expanded for loop?

We've seen simple numerical for loops before. For numerical lists these type of for loops well. What if we use a dictionary? a dictionary can also be used in a loop too!

Expanded For Loop

Given a dictionary with a one to one mapping we simply iterate over each item and print the key and value. We use the dictionaries method .items() which contains all items.

```
states = {
  'NY': 'New York',
  'ME': 'Maine',
  'VT': 'Vermont',
  'TX': 'Taxas',
  'LA': 'Los Angeles'
}

for key, value in states.items():
    print('Acronym: %s. State = %s ' % (key,value))
```

This will output:

```
Acronym: NY. State = New York
Acronym: ME. State = Maine
Acronym: VT. State = Vermont
Acronym: TX. State = Taxas
Acronym: LA. State = Los Angeles
```

What is going on? we used an expanded for loop. We

use both key and value through the dictionary states.

Read File

Reading files is straightforward: Python has built in support for reading and writing files. The function readlines() can be used to read the entire files contents.

Read file into list
We call the function method open to read the file, then we call the method readlines() to read all of the file contents into a variable. Finally we print out all file data.
Example read file:

```
#!/usr/bin/env python

filename = "readme.txt"

with open(filename) as fn:
    content = fn.readlines()

print(content)
```

Content will contain a list of all strings in the file.
If you print the variable content:

```
print(content)
```

you would see a list. Every item of the list contains

one line. However, every line of the list contains the newline character (\n).

To remove the newline characters from the list use:

content = [x.strip() for x in content]

Read file into string

If you want to read a file into a string variable, you can use a different method.
The code below reads the entire file data into a single string.

#!/usr/bin/env python

filename = "x.py"
contents = open(filename,'r').read()
print(contents)

Command line arguments
What are command line arguments in python?

In the command line, we can start a program with additional arguments.
These arguments are passed into the program.

Python programs can start with command line arguments. For example:

$ python program.py image.bmp

where program.py and image.bmp is are arguments. (the program is Python)

How to use command line arguments in python? We can use modules to get arguments.

Which modules can get command line arguments?

Note: Choose a module to get arguments. Examples below, try all!

If we set the last parameter to required=True, it has to be specified or it will throw an error.

Write file

Writing files is easy: Python has built in support for writing files. In this article we'll show you how to write data to a file.

To write a file, we must first open it. We can open the file with method open(filename, flag). The flag needs to be 'w', short for write.

Example code

We call the method open, then we write strings using the method write(). This is similar to how you would write files in other programming languages. Then we close the file.

To write files, you can use this code:
!/usr/bin/env python

```
f = open("output.txt","w")
f.write("Pythonprogramminglanguage.com, \n")
f.write("Example program.")
f.close()
```

On the first line we open the file for writing. The parameter "w" tells Python we want to open the file for writing. The write() calls write data into the file. Finally we close the file.

Write list to file
A list can be written directly into a file.
We do that by:

Define list
Open file
Write list elements using for loop
In code that's:

```
#!/usr/bin/env python

europe = [
'Netherlands','Belgium','France','Germany','Danmark]

mfile = open('europe.txt', 'w')
for country in europe:
  mfile.write("%s\n" % country)
```

Date and Time

Computers handle time using ticks. To get the date or time in Python we need to use the standard time module.

Note: All computers keep track of time since 12:00am, January 1, 1970, known as epoch time.

Epoch time

To get the number of ticks, use this program:

```
import time

ticks = time.time()
print("Ticks since epoch:", ticks)
```

The output will be similar to this:

Ticks since epoch: 1450535867.84

Local time
To get the current time on the machine, you can use the function localtime:

```
import time

timenow = time.localtime(time.time())
print("Current time :", timenow)
```

The output will not be formatted:

Current time : time.struct_time(tm_year=2015, tm_mon=12, tm_mday=19, tm_hour=15, tm_min=42, tm_sec=0, tm_wday=5, tm_yday=353, tm_isdst=0)
You can access each of the elements of the array:

```
import time

timenow = time.localtime(time.time())
print("Year:", timenow[0])
print("Month:", timenow[1])
print("Day:", timenow[2])
```

and use a combination for your own formatting. One alternative is to use the asctime function:

```
import time

timenow = time.asctime(time.localtime(time.time()))
print(timenow)
```

This will show output as:

Sat Dec 19 15:44:40 2015

Comments

Comments are little texts that can be added in code. They are created for programmers to read, not computers. A comment is simply one or more lines of text that is not executed by the computer.

There are two ways to comment in Python: single-line comments and multi-line comments.

Single line comment
A single line comment starts with the number sign (#) character:

```
# This is a comment
print('Hello')
```

For each line you want to comment, put the number sign (#) in front.

```
# print('This is not run')
print('Hello')
```

Comments should help other software developers, not be obvious like:

Multiline comment

Multiple lines can be created by repeating the number sign several times:

```
# This is a comment
# second line
x = 4
```

but this quickly becomes impractical. A common way

to use comments for multiple lines is to use the ("') symbol:

```
''' This is a multiline
Python comment example.'''
x = 5
```
How to install modules

Python modules allow you to use code of others in your code. This saves you a lot of development time, you don't have to reinvent the wheel each time.

There are two ways to install Python modules: system wide and using a virtual environment.

Virtualenv

We can create a virtual environemnt, that is seperate from the operating system. This allows you to use the same Python modules as other developers in your team.

Create a virtual environment with the line:

```
virtualenv foo
```
Then open /foo/

```
cd /foo/
```
You now have 3 directories: bin, include and lib.

Move up a directory.

To activate the virtual environment type:

source foo/bin/activate
we can then install any module, any version we want – without affecting the operating system. This way we can have the same version of modules as other developers.

Note: Pip will now install for this environment only.
To exit the virtual environment write:

deactivate

System wide
To install a module system wide, use pip and type

sudo pip install module-name
That will install a Python module automatically. Generally you do not install modules system wide.

Modules

What is a module? why?

A module is a Python file with one or more functions and variables. These functions and variables can be called from your program by importing a module.

Modules can be used to organize your code.

In this example we use the math module. This module has many functions such as sine, cosine as well as variables:

```
import math

print(math.pi)
x = math.sin(1)
print(x)
```

Find available functions and variables in a Python module
To find the available functions in a module, you can use this code:

```
import math

content = dir(math)
print(content)
```

A list will be returned with all functions and variables:

```
$ python example.py
['__doc__',   '__name__',   '__package__',   'acos',
'acosh', 'asin', 'asinh', 'atan', 'atan2', 'atanh',
'ceil', 'copysign', 'cos', 'cosh', 'degrees', 'e', 'erf',
'erfc', 'exp', 'expm1', 'fabs', 'factorial',
'floor', 'fmod', 'frexp', 'fsum', 'gamma', 'hypot', 'isinf',
'isnan', 'ldexp', 'lgamma', 'log', 'log10',
'log1p', 'modf', 'pi', 'pow', 'radians', 'sin', 'sinh', 'sqrt',
```

'tan', 'tanh', 'trunc']

Create your own module

First create a Python file with a function. We call this file hello.py and we have one function:

```
def hello():
    print("Hello World")
```

Now that we have create a module named hello we can use it in our program test.py

```
# Import your module
import hello

# Call of function defined in module
hello.hello()
```

Random Numbers

The random module can be used to make random numbers in Python. The function random() generates a number between 0 and 1.

Generate random nubers

Generate a real number between 0 and 1
Simply call the random() method to generate a real (float) number between 0 and 1.

```
import random
x = random.random()
print(x)
```

Generate a number between 0 and 50
We use the randint() method to generate a whole number.

```
import random
x = random.randint(0,50)
print(x)
```

Generate a random number between 1 and 10
Change the parameters of randint() to generate a number between 1 and 10.

```
import random
x = random.randint(1,10)
print(x)
```

List of random numbers
To generate a list of 100 random numbers:

```
import random

list = []

for i in range(0,100):
    x = random.randint(1,10)
    list.append(x)

print(list)
```

147

Choosing random items from a list
To get 3 random items from a list:

```
import random

list = [1,2,3,4,5,6,7,8,9,10]
x = random.sample(list,3)
print(x)
```

datetime

To print the current date, we can utilize the datetime module. Dates are objects, like anything in Python. Datetime has several subclasses, which can be confusing at first.

Date Example

We can use its method strftime() to change the format.
To show the current date (today):

```
import datetime
today = datetime.date.today()
print(today)
```
This will show the date in the format

YYYY-MM-DD
If you want another format, use the method strftime():

```
import datetime
today = datetime.date.today().strftime("%d-%m-%Y")
print(today)
```

This will output

DD-MM-YYYY
Get current time in Python
You can get the current time like this:

```
import datetime
currentTime = datetime.datetime.now().time()
print(currentTime)
```

To get the date and time, use:

```
import datetime
currentTime = datetime.datetime.now()
print(currentTime)
```

Format codes

When using the method strftime() we can specify the type of date format we want to show.
So which format codes do we have?

%a Locale's abbreviated weekday name.

%A Locale's full weekday name.

%b Locale's abbreviated month name.
%B Locale's full month name.

%c Locale's appropriate date and time representation.

%d Day of the month as a decimal number [01,31].

%f Microsecond as a decimal number [0,999999], zero-padded on the left

%H Hour (24-hour clock) as a decimal number [00,23].

%I Hour (12-hour clock) as a decimal number [01,12].

%j Day of the year as a decimal number [001,366].

%m Month as a decimal number [01,12].

%M Minute as a decimal number [00,59].

%p Locale's equivalent of either AM or PM.

%S Second as a decimal number [00,61].

%U Week number of the year (Sunday as the first day of the week)

%w Weekday as a decimal number [0(Sunday),6].

%W   Week number of the year (Monday as the first day of the week)

%x Locale's appropriate date representation.

%X Locale's appropriate time representation.

%y   Year without century as a decimal number [00,99].

%Y Year with century as a decimal number.

%z UTC offset in the form +HHMM or -HHMM.

%Z   Time zone name (empty string if the object is naive).

%% A literal '%' character.

Conclusion

Python is a popular choice for use as a scripting language for many software development processes. Similar to many other interpretative languages, Python offers more flexibility than compiled languages, and it can be efficiently used to integrate disparate systems together. Certainly, Python is a versatile programming language with several applications that are useful in diverse fields.